Mighty Machines
Police Cars

by Carol K. Lindeen

Consulting Editor: Gail Saunders-Smith, PhD

Capstone
press

Mankato, Minnesota

Pebble Plus is published by Capstone Press,
151 Good Counsel Drive, P.O. Box 669, Mankato, Minnesota 56002.
www.capstonepress.com

1 2 3 4 5 6 10 09 08 07 06 05

Library of Congress Cataloging-in-Publication Data
Lindeen, Carol K., 1976–
    Police cars / by Carol K. Lindeen.
    p. cm.—(Pebble plus: mighty machines)
    Includes bibliographical references and index.
    ISBN 0-7368-3654-3 (hardcover)
    ISBN 0-7368-5141-0 (softcover)
    1. Police vehicles—Juvenile literature. I. Title. II. Series.
HV7936.V4L56 2005
363.2'32—dc22   2004015065

Summary: Simple text and photographs present police cars, their parts, and how police officers use police cars.

Editorial Credits
Mari C. Schuh, editor; Molly Nei, set designer; Katie Opseth and Ted Williams, book designers;
  Jo Miller, photo researcher; Scott Thoms, photo editor

Photo Credits
Capstone Press/Karon Dubke, cover, 4–5
Daniel E. Hodges, 1, 9, 13
David R. Frazier Photolibrary, 18-19
The Image Finders, 10–11, 20-21; Mark E. Gibson, 14–15
Ron Kimball Stock, 6-7
Transparencies Inc., 17

Pebble Plus thanks the Mankato and North Mankato Police Departments for their assistance with photo shoots.

Note to Parents and Teachers

The Mighty Machines set supports national standards related to science, technology, and society. This book describes and illustrates police cars. The images support early readers in understanding the text. The repetition of words and phrases helps early readers learn new words. This book also introduces early readers to subject-specific vocabulary words, which are defined in the Glossary section. Early readers may need assistance to read some words and to use the Table of Contents, Glossary, Read More, Internet Sites, and Index sections of the book.

Table of Contents

What Are Police Cars?

Police cars are vehicles
that help police officers
do their jobs.

Police Car Parts

Police cars have sirens
and flashing lights.
They warn people that
a police car is in a hurry.

Police cars have radar.

Radar checks the speed

of passing cars.

Police cars have radios.
Police officers use radios
to call for help.

11

Police cars have computers.

Police officers look up

information on computers.

To the Rescue

A police officer

gets a call on the radio.

A car has crashed.

The police officer
turns on the sirens
and flashing lights.
The police car speeds
to the crash.

The police officer helps
the people at the crash.
He fills out a report
about the crash on
the police car's computer.

19

Police officers

use police cars

to help people

in emergencies.

Glossary

emergency—a sudden and dangerous situation; people need to deal with emergencies quickly.

police officer—a worker who helps keep people safe; police officers catch people who break the law.

radar—a tool that sends out electrical waves to find and keep track of something; police radar shows how fast other cars are moving.

siren—an object that makes a very loud sound as a warning

vehicle—something that carries people or goods from one place to another; police cars, ambulances, and fire trucks are types of vehicles.

Read More

Braithwaite, Jill. *Police Cars.* Pull Ahead Books. Minneapolis: Lerner, 2004.

Ethan, Eric. *Police Cars.* Emergency Vehicles. Milwaukee, Gareth Stevens, 2002.

Gordon, Sharon. *What's Inside a Police Car?* What's Inside? New York: Benchmark Books, 2004.

Internet Sites

FactHound offers a safe, fun way to find Internet sites related to this book. All of the sites on FactHound have been researched by our staff.

Here's how:

1. Visit *www.facthound.com*

2. Type in this special code **0736836543** for age-appropriate sites. Or enter a search word related to this book for a more general search.

3. Click on the **Fetch It** button.

FactHound will fetch the best sites for you!

Index

Word Count: 125
Grade: 1
Early-Intervention Level: 14